OPERA JOURNEYS LIBRETTO SERIES

Giacomo Puccini's

TURANDOT

COMPLETE LIBRETTO
with Music Highlight examples

Edited by Burton D. Fisher
Principal lecturer, *Opera Journeys Lecture Series*

Opera Journeys Publishing™/Boca Raton, Florida

WEB SITE: www.operajourneys.com

E MAIL: operaj@bellsouth.net

Libretto

Turandot

ACT I

*Ancient China. It is sunset in the Imperial City of Peking.
In a plaza before the Imperial Palace, there are large statuary of
sculptured monsters, unicorns, phoenixes and massive tortoises.
Hanging from an arch, there is a large bronze gong.
On the walls of the Palace are mounted
the severed heads of Turandot's failed suitors.
A Mandarin reads a decree to a large Crowd.*

Un mandarino

Popolo di Pekino! La legge è questa:
Turandot la Pura sposa sarà di chi,
di sangue regio,
spieghi i tre enigmi ch'ella proporrà.
Ma chi affronta il cimento e vinto resta
porga alla scure la superba testa!

A Mandarin

People of Peking! The law has stated:
the chaste Turandot will marry a man
of royal blood,
who solves the riddles that she proposes.
But the man who fails the test will have
his head impaled on the walls!

La folla

Ah! Ah!

The Crowd

Ah! Ah!

Il mandarino

Il principe di Persia avversa ebbe fortuna:
Al sorger della luna per la man del boia
muoia!

The Mandarin

The prince of Persia was unfortunate:
at moonrise, he will die by the
executioner's hand!

As the Mandarin departs, the crowd becomes rowdy and boisterous.

La folla

Muoia! Sì, muoia!
Noi vogliamo il carnefice!
Presto, presto! Muoia, Muoia!
Al supplizio! Muoia, muoia!
Presto, presto! Se non appari,
non ti sveglierem!
Pu-Tin-Pao, Pu-Tin-Pao!
Alla reggia! Alla reggia! Alla reggia!

The Crowd

Death! Yes, death!
We want the executioner!
Quickly, right away! Death!
To the torture! Death!
Quickly! If he doesn't appear,
we won't wake him!
Pu-Tin-Pao, Pu-Tin-Pao!
To the royal palace!

The Crowd moves toward the palace, shouting in fear and terror.
The guards repel them. In the clash, many people fall to the ground.

Le guardie imperiali
Indietro, cani! Indietro, cani!

Imperial Guards
Get back, you dogs!

La folla
Oh, crudeli! Pel cielo, fermi!
Oh, madre mia!

The Crowd
Oh, how cruel! For heaven's sake, stop!
Oh mother!

Le guardie imperiali
Indietro, cani!

Imperial Guards
Get back, you dogs!

La folla
Ahì! I miei bimbi! Crudeli!
Oh, madre mia! Crudeli!
Per il cielo, fermi! Fermi!
Fermi! Oh, madre mia!

The Crowd
Oh, my children! So cruel!
Oh, mother! So cruel!
For heaven's sake, stop!
Stop! Oh, mother!

Le guardie imperiali
Indietro, cani!

Imperial Guards
Get back, dogs!

Liù appears with the old and blind Timur.
After he falls to the ground, she cries in desperation for help.

Liù
Il mio vecchio è caduto!

Liù
The old man has fallen!

La folla
Crudeli! Siate umani! Pel cielo, fermi!
Crudeli! Non fateci male!

The Crowd *(to the Guards)*
So cruel! You are inhuman! For Heaven's
sake, stop! So cruel! Let's not be injured!

Le guardie imperiali
Indietro, cani!

Imperial Guards *(to the Crowd)*
Get back, dogs!

Liù
Chi m'aiuta a sorreggerlo?
Il mio vecchio è caduto. Pietà!

Liù
Who will help me to raise him?
The old man has fallen. Mercy!

Calaf appears and rushes to help Liù and Timur.
He recognizes his father, and shouts joyfully.

Calaf
Padre! Mio padre!

Calaf
Father! My father!

Le guardie imperiali
Indietro!

Imperial Guards
Get back!

Calaf
O padre, sì, ti ritrovo!

Calaf
Father, indeed I have found you!

La folla
Crudeli!

The Crowd
So cruel!

Calaf
Guardami! Non è sogno!

Calaf
Look at me! It isn't a dream!

La folla
Perché ci battete? Ahimè!

The Crowd
Why do you strike us? Mercy!

Liù
Mio signore!

Liù
My lord!

La folla
Pietà!

The Crowd
Mercy!

Calaf
Padre! Ascoltami! Padre! Son io!
E benedetto sia il dolor per questa gioia
che ci dona un Dio pietoso!

Calaf
Father! Listen to me! Father! It is me!
This is a painful joy, a blessing and a gift
from a merciful God!

Timur
O mio figlio! Tu! Vivo!

Timur
Oh my son! It is you! Alive!

Calaf
Taci! Chi usurpò la tua corona
me cerca e te persegue.
Non c'è asilo per noi, padre, nel mondo.

Calaf
Quiet! Those who usurped your throne
search and pursue you.
Father, there is no refuge in the world for us.

Timur
T'ho cercato, figlio mio, e t'ho creduto
morto.

Timur
I searched for you, my son, and I believed
that you were dead.

Calaf
T'ho pianto, padre, e bacio queste mani
sante.

Calaf
Father, I cried for you, and I kiss these
holy hands.

Timur
O figlio ritrovato!

Timur
My son, I have found you again!

As the Executioner's Servants arrive, the Crowd becomes agitated.
The Guards try to quiet the Crowd; they push them back, and try to disperse them.

La folla
Ecco i servi del boia.
Muoia! Muoia! Muoia! Muoia!

The Crowd
Here are the executioner's servants.
Death! Death! Death! Death!

Timur
Perduta la battaglia, vecchio re
senza regno e fuggente,
una voce sentii che mi diceva:
"Vien con me, sarò tua guida."
Era Liù.

Timur
The battle is lost. I am an old king,
a fugitive without a throne,
but I heard a voice saying to me:
"Come with me, I will lead you."
It was Liù.

Calaf
Sia benedetta!

Calaf
Bless her!

Timur
Ed io cadevo affranto, e m'asciugava il
pianto, mendicava per me.

Timur
I was crushed. She dried my tears,
and sought alms for me.

Calaf
Liù, chi sei?

Calaf
Liù, who are you?

Liù
Nulla sono! Una schiava, mio signore.

Liù *(humbly)*
My lord, I am nothing, just a slave.

The Executioner's Servants sharpen their blades on the flint stones.

Le donne, gli uomini
Gira la cote!

Women and Men
The sharpening stone turns!

Calaf
E perché tanta angoscia hai diviso?

Calaf
Why have you suffered so much anguish?

Liù
Perché un dì nella reggia m'hai sorriso.

Liù
Because one day, in the royal palace,
you smiled upon me.

Gli uomini
Gira la cote, gira, gira! Gira, gira, gira!

The Men
The sharpening stone turns! It turns!

I servi del boia
Ungi, arrota, che la lama guizzi,
sprizzi fuoco e sangue!
Il lavoro mai non langue, mai non langue.

The Executioner's servants
Grease and hone the blade so that it
glistens, and spouts fire and blood!
The work of the executioner never ends.

La folla
…mai non langue…

The Crowd
…it never ends...

I servi del boia
…dove regna Turandot.

The Executioner's servants
…where Turandot reigns.

La folla
…dove regna Turandot.

The Crowd
…where Turandot reigns.

I servi del boia
Ingi! Arrota!

The Executioner's servants
Grease and hone the blade!

I servi del boia, gli uomini
Fuoco e sangue!

Executioner's servants, the Men
Fire and blood!

Le donne, gli uomini
Dolci amanti, avanti, avanti!

Woman and Men
Gentle lovers, come forward!

I servi del boia
Cogli uncini e coi coltelli

The Executioner's servants
With hooks and the knives.

Gli uomini
Noi siam pronti a ricamar le vostre pelli!

Men
We are ready to weave your hair!

La folla
Dolci amanti, avanti, avanti!

The Crowd
Gentle lovers, come forward!

I servi del boia
Siamo pronti a ricamar!

The Executioner's servants
We are ready to weave!

Tutti
Chi quel gong percuoterà apparire la vedrà!
Bianca al pari della giada,
fredda come quella spada
é la bella Turandot!

All
Whoever strikes the gong will see her
appear! The beautiful Turandot
is pure like jade,
but cold like that saber!

Dolci amanti, avanti, avanti!
Quando rangola il gong gongola il boia.
Vano è l'amore se non c'è fortuna.
Gli enigmi sono tre, la morte è una!
La morte è una! Ungi, arrota!

Gentle lovers, come forward!
When the gong sound, the executioner
rejoices. Love is futile without luck!
There are three enigmas, but one death!
Grease and hone the blade!

La folla

Gli enigmi sono tre, la morte è una!
Che la lama guizzi, sprizzi sangue.
Chi quel gong percuoterà?

The Crowd

There are three enigmas, but one death!
May the blade glisten and spout blood.
Who will strike the gong?

I servi del boia

Morte! Morte!

The Executioner's Servants

Death! Death!

La folla

Ah, ah! Ah, ah!

The Crowd

Hah, hah! Hah, hah!

I servi del boia, la folla

...dove regna Turandot!

The Executioner's Servants, the Crowd

...where Turandot reigns!

The Servants leave to deliver the sharpened blade to the Executioner.
The Crowd looks toward the sky, which slowly darkens.

La folla

Perché tarda la luna? Faccia pallida!
Mostrati in cielo! Presto, vieni!
Spunta! O testa mozza! O squallida!
Vieni! Spunta! Mostrati in cielo!
O testa mozza! O esangue!
O esangue, o squallida!
O taciturna! O amante, smunta dei morti!
O taciturna, mostrati in cielo!
Come aspettano, o taciturna,
il tuo funereo, lume i cimiteri!
O esangue, squallida!
O testa mozza!

The Crowd

Why is the moon so late? Pale face!
Show yourself in the sky! Quickly, come!
Emerge! Severed head! Wretched face!
Come! Emerge! Show yourself in the sky!
Oh severed head! Oh colorless face!
Oh colorless face, oh wretched face!
Oh silent one! Oh lover, pale from death!
Oh silent one, show yourself in the sky!
How they wait, oh silent one,
for your funeral, graveyard light!
Oh colorless face, wretched face!
Oh severed head!

Ecco laggiù un barlume!
Vieni, presto, spunta!
O testa mozza, spunta!
Vieni! O testa mozza, vieni!
Mostrati, o faccia pallida!
O faccia pallida! O esangue, pallida!
Vieni, amante smunta dei morti!
O amante, smunta dei morti!
Vieni, vieni, spunta!

There is a glitter over there!
Come, quickly, emerge!
Oh severed head, emerge!
Come! Oh severed head, come!
Show yourself, oh colorless face!
Oh pale face! Oh colorless face!
Come, lover pale from death!
Oh lover, pale from death!
Come, come, emerge!

The moon begins to appear

Ecco laggiù un barlume, dilaga in cielo,
la sua luce smorta!

There is a glitter over there, your pallid
light floods the sky!

Tutti	**All**
Pu-Tin-Pao! La luna è smorta!	Pu-Tin-Pao! The moon is pallid!
Ragazzi	**Boys**
Là sui monti dell'Est la cicogna cantò.	There, in the eastern mountains, the stork sang.
Ma l'april non rifiorì, ma la neve non sgelò.	But in April there was no flowering, because the snow did not melt.
Dal deserto al mar non odi tu mille voci sospirar:	From desert to sea, you failed to hear thousands of sighing voices calling to you:
"Principessa, scendi a me!	"Princess, descend to me!
Tutto fiorirà, tutto splenderà!"	All will bloom, all will be resplendent!"
Ah!	Ah!

A cortege accompanies the Prince of Persia to the scaffold.
As the crowd notices that he is pallid and dazed,
their fierce and barbarous demeanor transforms to pity and compassion.

La folla	**The Crowd**
O giovinetto! Grazia, grazia!	Such a young man! Mercy and pity!
Com'è fermo il suo passo! Grazia!	How firm his steps are! Mercy!
Com'è dolce, com'è dolce il suo volto!	How gentle his face is!
Ha negli occhi l'ebbrezza! Pietà!	His eyes are dreamy! Mercy!
Com'è fermo il suo passo!	How firm his steps are!
Ha negli occhi la gioia! Pietà! Pietà!	He has joy in his eyes! Mercy! Mercy!
Calaf	**Calaf**
Ah! La grazia!	Oh! Mercy!
Le donne, gli uomini, la folla	**Women, Men, and the Crowd**
Pietà di lui! Pietà! Principessa!	Mercy on him! Mercy! Princess!
Pietà di lui! Pietà!	Mercy on him! Mercy!
Principessa! Grazia! Grazia!	Princess! Mercy and pity!
Pietà di lui! Pietà! Pietà!	Mercy on him! Mercy! Mercy!
Calaf	**Calaf** *(addressing Turandot)*
Ch'io ti veda e ch'io ti maledica!	If I could see you I would curse you!
Crudele, ch'io ti maledica!	You are so cruel, that I would curse you!
La folla, gli uomini	**The Crowd, the Men**
Principessa! Pietà di lui!	Princess! Mercy on him!
Principessa! Principessa, pietà!	Princess! Princess, mercy!
Principessa! Pietà di lui! Pietà di lui!	Princess! Mercy on him! Mercy on him!
Pietà! Pietà! La grazia, Principessa!	Mercy! Mercy! Mercy! Princess!
Principessa! La grazia! La grazia!	Princess! Mercy! Mercy!

*The Crowd turns toward a balcony where Turandot appears like a vision,
illuminated by a ray of moonlight.
The Crowd kneels in supplication; only standing are Calaf,
the Executioner, and the Prince of Persia.
Turandot makes an imperious gesture indicating that the
Prince of Persia is to be condemned to death.*

Calaf becomes intoxicated by the vision of Turandot.

Calaf
O divina belezza!
O meraviglia! O sogno!

Calaf
Oh what a divine beauty!
Oh what a marvel! Oh what a dream!

I sacerdoti bianchi del corteo
O gran Koung-tzè!
Che lo spirito del morente giunga fino a te!

Priests
Oh great Koung-tzè!
May the spirit of the dying join you!

*All disperse. In the semidarkness before the palace,
only Calaf, Liù and Timur remain.
Timur approaches Calaf and admonishes his son's impetuosity.*

Timur
Figlio, che fai?

Timur
My son, what are you doing?

Calaf
Non senti? Il suo profumo è nell'aria!
È nell'anima!

Calaf
Don't you understand? Her perfume is in the air! It has penetrated my soul!

Timur
Ti perdi!

Timur
You have lost yourself!

Calaf
O divina belezza, meraviglia!
Io soffro, padre, soffro!

Calaf
Oh what a divine and marvelous beauty!
Father, I am suffering!

Timur
No, no! Stringiti a me.
Liù, parlagli tu!
Qui salvezza non c'è!
Prendi nella tua mano la sua mano!

Timur
No, no! Embrace me.
Liù, you speak to him too!
There is no safety here!
Take his hand in yours!

Liù
Signore, andiam lontano!

Liù
My lord, let's go far away!

Timur
La vita c'è laggiù!

Timur
Life is over far away!

Calaf
Quest'è la vita, padre!

Calaf
Father, here is where life is!

Timur
La vita c'è laggiù!

Timur
Life for us is far away from here!

Calaf
Io soffro, padre, soffro!

Calaf
Father, I am suffering!

Timur
Qui salvezza non c'è!

Timur
There is no safety here!

Calaf
La vita, padre, è qui!
Turandot! Turandot! Turandot!

Calaf
Father, life is here!
Turandot! Turandot! Turandot!

Just before his beheading, the Prince of Persia
is heard shouting the name of Turandot.

La voce del principe del Persia
Turandot!

The Prince of Persia
Turandot!

La folla
Ah!

The Crowd
Ah!

Timur
Vuoi morire così?

Timur
Do you want to die that way?

Calaf
Vincere, padre, nella sua belezza!

Calaf
Father, I will win her beauty!

Timur
Vuoi finire così?

Timur
Do you want to end that way?

Calaf   **Calaf**
Vincere gloriosamente nella sua bellezza!   I will win her beauty with glory!

As Calaf advances toward the gong to challenge Turandot's riddles,
Turandot's Three Ministers block his path.

Ping, Pong, Pang   **Ping, Pong, Pang**
Fermo! Che fai? T'arresta!   Halt! What are you doing? Stop!
Chi sei, che fai, che vuoi?   Who are you, what are you doing, what do
Va' via!   you want? Go away!
Va', la porta è questa   Go, this is the door
della gran beccheria!   to a large butchershop!

Pazzo, va' via!   Insane man, go away!
Qui si strozza! Si trivella! Si sgozza!   Here one is strangled! Stabbed! Slaughtered!
Si spella! Si uncina e scapitozza!   Skinned! The head impaled!
Va' via! Si sega e si sbudella! Va' via!   Go away! One is sawed and disemboweled!
Sollecito, precipite.Va' via!   Hurry, quickly. Go away!

Al tuo paese torna in cerco d'uno stipite.   Return to your country and family.
Che vuoi, chi sei?   What do you want, who are you?
Per romperti la corona!   You want to destroy the crown!
Va' via, va' via!   Go away!
Ma qui no!   Not here!
Pazzo, va' via, va' via!   Insane man, go away!

Calaf   **Calaf** *(trying to reach the gong)*
Lasciatemi passare!   Let me pass!

Ping, Pong, Pang   **Ping, Pong, Pang**
Qui tutti i cimiteri sono occupati!   Here all the cemeteries are full!
Qui bastano i pazzi indigeni!   Here there are enough insane people!
Non vogliam più pazzi forestieri!   We don't want more insane foreigners!
O scappi, o il funeral per te s'appressa!   Run away, or your funeral awaits you!

Calaf   **Calaf**
Lasciatemi passare!   Let me pass!

Ping, Pong, Pang   **Ping, Pong, Pang**
Per una principessa! Peuh! Che cos'è?   All for a Princess! Ay! What is she?
Una femmina colla corona in testa   A woman with a crown on her head
e il manto colla frangia!   and a fringed dress.
Ma se la spogli nuda è carne!   But if you undress her she is flesh!
È carne cruda! È roba che non si mangia!   Impure flesh! Something not to be eaten!

Calaf
Lasciatemi passare, lasciatemi!

Calaf
Let me pass, let me pass!

Ping, Pong, Pang
Ah, ah, ah!

Ping, Pong, Pang
Ha, ha, ha!

Ping
Lascia le donne! O prendi cento spose,
che, in fondo, la più sublime Turandot del
mondo ha una faccia, due braccia, e due
gambe, sì belle, imperiali, sì, sì,
belle, ma sempre quelle!

Ping *(calmly and with quiet dignity)*
Leave the women! It is better to take one
hundred wives that are more splendid than
Turandot, with a face, two arms, and two
legs. Yes, yes, very beautiful women who
are very regal and beautiful, but only take
those!

Con cento mogli, o sciocco,
avrai gambe di ribocco,
duecento braccia e cento dolci petti.

With one hundred wives, foolish man,
you'll have legs overflowing, two hundred
arms and one hundred gentle breasts.

Ping, Pong, Pang
Cento petti sparsi per cento letti!
Ah, ah, ah!

Ping, Pong, Pang
One hundred breasts for one hundred beds!
Ha, ha, ha!

Calaf
Lasciatemi passar!

Calaf
Let me pass!

Ping, Pong, Pang
Pazzo, va' via, va' via!

Ping, Pong, Pang
Insane man, go away!

Turandot's Servants appear on the balcony of the Imperial Palace
and raise their hands to silence the noise.

Le ancelle di Turandot
Silenzio, olà! Laggiù chi parla? Silenzio!
Silenzio! È l'ora dolcissima del sonno.
Silenzio, silenzio, silenzio!
Il sonno sfiora gli occhi di Turandot!
Si profuma di lei l'oscurità!

Turandot's Servants
Silence over there! Who's talking over
there? Quiet! It is the time for her gentle
sleep. Quiet, quiet, quiet!
Turandot's eyes have just barely closed!
Her fragrance has disappeared!

Ping
Via di là, femmine ciarliere!

Ping
Leave here, and the feminine chatter!

Ping, Pong, Pang
Attenti al gong! Attenti al gong!

Ping, Pong, Pang
Listen to the gong!

Calaf
Si profuma di lei l'oscurità!

Calaf
Her fragrance has disappeared!

Ping, Pong, Pang
Guardalo, Pong (Ping, Pang)!
È insordito! Intontito! Allucinato!

Ping, Pong, Pang
Look at him, Pong (Ping, Pang)!
He's deaf! Stupefied! Hallucinated!

Timur
Più non li ascolta, ahimè!

Timur
I can't bear to listen any more!

Ping, Pong, Pang
Su! Parliamogli in tre!
Notte senza lumicino, gola nero d'un
cammino son più chiare degli enigmi di
Turandot!

Ping, Pong, Pang
Get up! Let's speak to him together!
A dark, unlit road at night,
is much clearer
than Turandot's enigmas!

Ferro, bronzo, muro, roccia,
l'ostinata tua capoccia,
son men duri degli enigmi di Turandot!
Dunque va', saluta tutti!
Varca i monti, taglia i flutti!
Sta alla larga dagli enigmi di Turandot!

Steel, bronze, walls, rocks,
are obstacles in your path that are less
difficult than Turandot's riddles!
Wherever you go, everyone greets you!
Across the mountains, cutting the waves!
But stay far away from Turandot's riddles!

Voices from the impaled heads of Turandot's failed victims.

Le ombre dei morti
Non indugiare!
Se chiami, appare quella che estinti ci fa
sognare.
Fa ch'ella parli!
Fa che l'udiamo! Io l'amo!
Io l'amo! Io l'amo!

Apparitions of the dead
Don't delay!
If you call, the dead appear in your
dreams.
Make her talk to you!
Make her listen! I love you!
I love you! I love you!

Calaf
No, no, io solo l'amo!

Calaf
No, no, I alone love her!

Ping, Pong, Pang
L'ami? Che cosa?
Chi? Turandot?
Ah, ah, ah! Turandot!
O ragazzo demente!
Turandot non esiste!
Non esiste che il niente nel quale ti
annulli!
Turandot non esiste, non esiste!
Come tutti quei citrulli tuoi pari!
L'uomo! Il Dio! Io! I popoli! I sovrani!
Pu-Tin-Pao! Non esiste che il Tao!

Ping, Pong, Pang
You love her? What is this?
Who? Turandot?
Ha, ha, ha! Turandot!
Oh insane young man!
Turandot doesn't exist!
She doesn't exist at all,
 so call off your quest!
Turandot doesn't exist!
You are the same as all those other fools!
Man! God! Me! People! Subjects!
Pu-Tin-Pao! The Tao doesn't exist!

Tu ti annulli come quei citrulli tuoi pari,
tu ti annulli!
Come tutti quei citrulli tuoi pari!
Non esiste che il Tao!

End your quest or you'll die like all those
other fools, end your quest!
You are like all those other fools!
The only reality is the executioner!

Calaf
A me il trionfo!
A me l'amore!

Calaf
It will be my triumph!
Her love will be mine!!

The Executioner appears with the severed head of the Prince of Persia.

Ping, Pong, Pang
Stolto, ecco l'amore!
Così la luna bacerà il tuo volto!

Ping, Pong, Pang *(pointing to the head)*
Fool, that is love!
That is the light that will kiss your face!

TImur addresses Calaf with desperate supplication.

Timur
O figlio, vuoi dunque ch'io solo trascini
pel mondo la mia torturata vecchiezza?
Aiuto! Non c'è voce umana
che muova il tuo cuore feroce?

Timur
My son, do you want me to roam the
world alone, like a tortured old man?
Help me! Is there a human voice that can
penetrate your ferocious heart?

Signore a - scolta! Ah, signore, ascolta!

Liù
Signore, ascolta! Ah, signore, ascolta!
Liù non regge più, si spezza il cuor!
Ahimè, quanto cammino col tuo nome
nell'anima,
col nome tuo sulle labbra!
Ma se il tuo destino doman sarà deciso,
noi morrem sulla strada dell'esilio.
Ei perderà suo figlio, io l'ombra d'un
sorriso.
Liù non regge più! Ah!

Liù
My lord, listen to me! My lord, listen!
Liù can bear it no longer, her heart breaks!
Alas, how many roads I traveled with your
name in my soul,
with your name on my lips!
But if you have decided that tomorrow
holds your destiny, we'll die in exile.
He will lose his son, and I will lose the
trace of a smile.
Liù can bear it no longer! Ah!

A tempo rallentando
CALAF

Non piangere, Liù!   *Se in un lontano giorno io t'ho*   *sorriso*

Calaf
Non piangere, Liù!
Se in un lontano giorno io t'ho sorriso,
per quel sorriso, dolce mia fanciulla,
m'ascolta:
il tuo signore sarà domani, forse solo al mondo.
Non lo lasciare, portalo via con te!

Calaf
Don't cry, Liù!
If a long time ago I smiled upon you,
it is because of that smile, gentle little girl,
that you must wait for me:
perhaps you are alone in the world, but
your man will come to you tomorrow..
No don't leave him, take him with you!

Liù
Noi morrem sulla strada dell'esilio!

Liù
We'll die in exile!

Timur
Noi morrem!

Timur
We will die!

Calaf
Dell'esilio addolcisci a lui le strade!
Questo, o mia povera Liù,
al tuo piccolo cuore che non cade,
chiede colui che non sorride più!

Calaf
Sweeten the road of his exile!
My poor little Liù,
your little heart should not fail to
be with him or he will no longer smile!

Andante sostenuto

Timur
Ah, per l'ultima volta!

Timur
Ah, for the last time!

Liù
Vinci il fascino orribile!

Liù
I am defeated by his horrible charm!

Ping, Pong, Pang
La vita è così bella!

Ping, Pong, Pang
Life is so beautiful!

Timur
Abbi di me pietà!

Timur
Have mercy on me!

Liù
Abbi di Liù pietà!

Liù
Have mercy on me!

Timur
Abbi di me, di me pietà, pietà!

Timur
Have mercy on me, mercy!

Ping, Pong, Pang
Non perderti così!

Ping, Pong, Pang
Don't destroy yourself this way!

Calaf
Son io che domando pietà!

Calaf
It is I who asks mercy!

Liù
Signore, pietà!

Liù
My lord, mercy!

Timur
Non posso staccarmi da te!

Timur
I cannot leave without you!

Calaf
Nessuno più ascolto! Nessuno più ascolto!

Calaf
No one wait here any more!

Liù
Pietà di lui!

Liù
Mercy for him!

Ping, Pong, Pang
Afferralo, portalo via! Portalo via!
Su! Porta via quel pazzo!

Ping, Pong, Pang
Grab him, and take him away!
Get up! Take this insane man away!

Calaf
Io vedo il suo fulgido volto!
La vedo! Mi chiama! Essa è là!
Il tuo perdono chiede colui che non
sorride più!

Calaf
I see her resplendent face!
I see it! She calls me! She is there!
I ask for your pardon because you can no
longer smile!

Timur
Non voglio staccarmi da te! Pietà! Pietà!
Mi getto ai tuoi piedi gemente.
Abbi pietà! Non voler la mia morte!

Timur
I cannot leave you! Mercy! Mercy!
I throw myself at your feet lamenting.
Have mercy! Don't wish my death!

Ping, Pong, Pang
Su, portalo via quel pazzo!
Trattieni quel pazzo furente!
Folle tu sei! La vita è bella!

Ping, Pong, Pang
Get up! Take this insane man away!
Hold on to this furious insane man!
You are foolish! Life is beautiful!

Liù
Pietà! Signore, pietà, pietà!

Liù
Mercy! Lord, mercy, mercy!

Ping, Pong, Pang
Su, un ultimo sforzo, portiamolo via!
Portiamolo via, portiamolo via!

Ping, Pong, Pang
Up, a last effort, let's take him away!
Let's take him away!

Calaf
Lasciatemi! Ho troppo sofferto!
La gloria m'aspetta laggiù.
Forza umana non c'è che mi trattenga.
Io seguo la mia sorte.
Son tutto una febbre, son tutto un delirio!
Ogni senso è un martirio feroce.
Ogni fibra dell'anima ha una voce che
grida: Turandot.

Calaf
Let me alone! I have suffered too much!
My glory awaits me there.
There is no human force that can hold me.
I follow my destiny.
I am inflamed, delirious!
I feel a sense of fierce torture.
Every fiber in my soul is shouting:
Turandot.

Timur
Tu passi su un povero core
che sanguina invano per te!
Nessuno ha mai vinto, nessuno.
Su tutti la spiada piombò.
Mi getto ai tuoi piedi: non voler la mia
morte!

Timur
You are stepping upon a poor heart that
hopes for you in vain!
No one has ever been victorious, no one.
The deadly ghost has fallen on all of us.
I throw myself at your feet: you do not
wish me to die!

Ping, Pong, Pang
Il volto che vedi è illusione,
la luce che splende è funesta.
Tu giochi la tua perdizione, tu giochi la
testa.
La morte, c'è l'ombra del bioa laggiù.
Tu corri alla rovina!
La vita non giocar!

Ping, Pong, Pang
The face that you see is an illusion,
the light that shines is deadly.
You are playing with hell, you are
gambling with your head.
Death, there in the shadow of the executioner.
You are running to your ruin!
Don't play games with life!

Liù
Pietà! Pietà di noi!
Se questo suo strazio non basta,
signore, noi siamo perduti con te!
Ah, fuggiamo, signore, ah! Fuggiamo!

Liù
Mercy! Mercy on us!
If this torture is not enough, my lord,
we are lost with you!
Ah, let's flee, my lord! Let's flee!

La folla
La fossa già scaviam per te che vuoi sfidar
l'amor.
Nel buio c'è segnato, ahimè, il tuo crudel
destin!

The Crowd
We'll dig the grave for you if you wish to
challenge love.
The executioner is the sign of your cruel
destiny!

Calaf
Turandot!

Calaf
Turandot!

Calaf strikes the gong three times.

Liù, Timur, Ping, Pong, Pang
La morte!

Liù, Timur, Ping, Pong, Pang
Death!

Calaf

Turandot!

Calaf
Turandot!

Ping, Pong, Pang
E lasciamolo andar! Inutile è gridar in
sanscritto, in cinese, in lingua mongola!
Quando rangola il gong la morte gangola.
Ah, ah, ah, ah!

Ping, Pong, Pang
Let's let him go! It's useless to shout in
either Sanskrit, Chinese, or Mongolian!
When the gong is struck, death resounds.
Ha, ha, ha, ha!

Calaf remains in ecstasy at the base of the gong.
Liù and Timur embrace each other as they look at him despairingly.

ACT II - Scene I

A Pavilion decorated with symbolic and fantastic Chinese figures.
Turandot's Three Ministers, Ping, Pang, and Pong,
philosophize pessimistically about events in the realm.

Ping
Olà, Pang! Olà, Pong!
Poiché il funesto gong desta la reggia e
desta la città, siam pronti ad ogni evento:
Se lo straniero vince, per le nozze,
e s'egli perde, pel seppellimento.

Ping
Hello, Pang! Hello, Pong!
Since the solemn gong awakened the
empire, every city has become stirred.
We are ready for every event: the wedding
if the stranger wins, and the burial if he
loses.

Ping, Pong, Pang
Io preparo le nozze, ed io le esequie,
Le rosse lanterne di festa!
Le bianche lanterne di lutto!
Gli incensi e le offerte,
monete di carta dorate,
il bel palanchino scarlatto, thè, zuccero,
noci moscate, il feretro grande,
ben fatto, i bonzi che cantano,
i bonzi che gemono,
e tutto quanto il resto, secondo vuole il
rito, minuzioso, infinito!

Ping, Pong, Pang
I prepare weddings, and I prepare funerals,
The red lanterns for a party!
The white lanterns for mourning!
The incense and the offerings,
moneys for gilded paper,
a beautiful scarlet carriage, tea, sugar,
walnut, wine, a well-made grand coffin,
and priests who sing,
and priests who groan,
and everything else for the second wish of
the rite, will be meticulous and endless!

Ping
O China, o China, che or sussulti
e trasecoli inquieta,
come dormivi lieta, gonfia
dei tuoi settantamila secoli!

Ping
Oh China, oh China, you are shaking and
startled into restlessness,
how you slept happily, arrogant from
your seventeen thousand centuries.

Ping, Pong, Pang
Tutto andava secondo
l'antichissima regola del mondo.
Poi nacque Turandot.
E sono anni che le nostre feste
si riducono a gioie come queste:
tre battute di gong, tre indovinelli,
e giù teste!

Ping, Pong, Pang
All was going favorably for the
oldest empire in the world.
Then Turandot was born.
And in these years the joys of our feasts
have dwindled:
three strikes of the gong, three puzzles,
and then heads!

L'anno del topo furon sei.
L'anno del cane furon otto.
Nell'anno in corso, il terribile anno della Tigre.
Siamo già al tredicesimo!
Tredicesimo, con quello che va sotto!
Che lavoro! Che noia!
A che siamo mai ridotti?
I ministri siam del boia!
Ministri del boia!

There were six years of the sign of the rat.
There were eights years of the dog.
And in the course of years, the terrible year of the tiger.
We already have the thirteenth!
Thirteenth, with the earlier ones!
What work! What bother!
And why have we been demoted?
We are ministers of the executioner!
Ministers of the executioner!

Andante mosso

Ho una ca - sa nell'Ho - nan   con il   suo laghet - to   blù,

Ping

Ho una casa nell'Honan con il suo laghetto blu, tutto cinto di bambù.
E sto qui a dissiparmi la mia vita, a stillarmi il cervel sui libri sacri.

Ping

I have a house in Hunan with a blue lake, all made with bamboo.
Here my life becomes dissipated, racking my brains with sacred books.

Ping, Pong, Pang

Sui libri sacri. E potrei tornar laggiù, presso il mio laghetto blu, tutto cinto di bambù.

Ping, Pong, Pang

Sacred books. If I could only return there, to my blue lake that is surrounded with bamboo.

Pong

Ho foreste, presso Tsiang, che più belle non c'è ne,
che non hanno ombra per me.
Ho foreste, che più belle non c'è ne!

Pong

I have a forest near Tsiang, and there is nothing more beautiful,
that could arouse my imagination.
I have a forest, and nothing is more beautiful!

Pang

Ho un giardino, presso Kiu, che lasciai per venir qui, e che non rivedrò, non rivedrò mai più, mai più!

Pang

I have a garden near Kiu, that I left to come here,
and that I'll never see again, never again!

Ping

E potrei tornar laggiù, presso mio laghetto blu, tutto cinto di bambù!

Ping

That I might be able to return there, near my blue lake, all surrounded with bamboo.

Ping, Pong, Pang
E stiam qui a stillarci il cervel, sui libri
sacri!
E potrei tornare a Tsiang.
E potrei tornare laggiù. E potrei tornare a
Kiu,
a godermi il lago blu. Tsiang...Kiu...
Honan...tutto cinto di bambù!

Ping, Pong, Pang
Here we rack our brains with sacred books!

If I could return to Tsiang.
If I could return there. And I could return
to the sea at Kiu,
and enjoy the blue lake. Tsiang...Kiu...
Honan...all surrounded by bamboo!

Ping, Pong, Pang
O mondo pieno di pazzi innamorati!
Ne abbiam visti arrivar degli aspiranti!
O quanti! O quanti!

Ping, Pong, Pang
Oh world full of insane lovers!
We have seen the candidates arrive!
Oh so many! So many!

Ping
O mondo pieno di pazzi innamorati!
Vi ricordate il principe regal di
Samarcanda?
Fece la sua domanda,
e lei con quale gioia gli mandò il boia!

Ping
Oh world full of insane lovers!
Do you remember the royal prince of
Samarcanda?
She posed her question,
and she sent him joyfully to the
executioner!

La folla
Ungi, arrota, che la lama guizzi e sprizzi
fuoco e sangue!

The Crowd *(from outside)*
Sharpen and hone the blade so that fire and
blood will gush forth!

Ping, Pong, Pang
Il boia! E l'Indiano gemmato Sagarika
cogli orecchini come campanelli?
Amore chiese, fu decapitato!
Ed il Birmano? E il prence dei Kirghisi?
Uccisi! Uccisi! Uccisi! Uccisi!
E il Tartaro dall'arco di sei cubiti
di ricche pelli cinto? Estinto! Estinto!

Ping, Pong, Pang
The executioner! And the jeweled Sagarika
Indian with little ears like bells?
He wanted love and was decapitated!
And the Burmese? And the prince of Kirghis?
Killed! Killed! Killed! Killed!
And the Tartar skinned by an arrow from
six cubits? Exterminated! Exterminated!

La folla
Dove regna Turandot il lavoro mai non
langue!

The Crowd
Where Turandot reigns the work never
ends!

Ping, Pong, Pang
E decapita! Uccidi! Uccidi!
Uccidi! Uccidi! Ammazza!
Estingui! Uccidi!
Estingui! Ammazza!

Ping, Pong, Pang
Decapitated! Killed! Killed!
Killed! Killed! Murdered!
Exterminated! Killed!
Exterminated! Murdered!

Addio, amore, addio, razza!   Farewell love, farewell race!
Addio, stirpe divina!   Farewell divine culture!
E finisce la China!   China is finished!
Addio, stirpe divina!   Farewell divine culture!
O Tigre! O Tigre!   Oh Tiger! Oh Tiger!

O grande marescialla del cielo,   Oh great lord of the sky,
fa che giunga la gran notte attesa,   make the anticipated great night arrive,
la notte della resa!   the night of surrender!
Il talamo le voglio preparare!   I want to prepare the nuptial bed for her!
Sprimaccerò per lei le molli piume.   I will fluff the soft feathers.
Io l'alcova le voglio profumare.   I will perfume the bedroom.
Gli sposi guiderò reggendo il lume.   I will guide the newlyweds with light.
Poi tutt'e tre in giardino noi canterem   Then the three of us will sing in the garden
d'amor   about love
fino al mattino, così.   until morning, just like this.

Non v'è in China per nostra fortuna   Our fate is that there has never before been
donna più che rinneghi l'amor!   a woman in China who repudiated love!
Una sola ce n'era e quest'una che fu   Only one, and that one was ice,
ghiaccio, ora è vampa ed ardor!   and now it has flame and ardor!

Principessa, il tuo impero si stende   Princess, your empire extends from Tsè-
dal Tsè-Kiang all'immenso Jang-Tsè!   Kiang to the vast Yangtse!
Ma là, dentro alle soffici tende,   But there, behind the soft tents,
c'è uno sposo che impera su te!   there is a man who wants to rule you!
Tu dei baci già senti l'aroma,   He has already sensed the aroma of your
già sei doma, sei tutta languor!   kisses, you are already tamed, and you are
        already weakening!

Gloria, gloria alla notte segreta,   Glory, glory to the secret night,
che il prodigio ora vede compir!   that the wonder might be fulfilled now!
Gloria, gloria alla gialla coperta di seta,   Glory, glory to the yellow cover of silk,
notte segreta!   secret night!
Testimonio dei dolci sospir!   Witness of gentle sighs!

Nel giardin sussurran le cose   In the garden things murmur
e tintinnan campanule d'or.   and golden flowers jingle.
Si sospiran parole amorose,   Sighing words of love,
di rugiada s'imperlano i fior!   make the dew cover the flowers!
Gloria, gloria al bel corpo discinto   Glory, glory to the mysteries of that
che il mistero ignorato ora sa!   scantily dressed body that no one knows!
Gloria all'ebbrezza e all'amore   Glory to intoxication and to love,
che ha vinto e alla China la pace ridà!   that it may triumph and China may smile
        in peace!

Ping

Noi si sogna e il palazzo già formicola di
lanterne, di servi e di soldati.
Udite il gran tamburo del tempio verde!
Già stridon le infinite ciabatte di Pekino.

Ping

We rest while the palace is already filling
with lanterns, servants and soldiers.
Listen to the great drum from the green
temple! The multitudes of Peking are
already striding to the palace.

Ping, Pong, Pang

Udite trombe! Altro che pace!
Ha inizio la ceremonia.
Andiamo a goderci l'ennesimo supplizio!

Ping, Pong, Pang

Hear the trumpets! No more peace!
The ceremony has begun!
Let's go enjoy the ultimate torture!

ACT II - Scene 2

A plaza before the Royal Palace.
Large steps lead up to a throne in which the Emperor Altoum is seated.
The Mandarin ceremoniously arrives, followed by eight Wisemen, who bear scrolls
with the answers to Turandot's enigmas.
The Three Ministers arrive, and the Crowd slowly fills the plaza.

La folla

Gravi, enormi ed imponenti col mister dei
chiusi enigmi
già s'avanzano i sapienti.
Ecco Ping! Ecco Pong! Ecco Pang!

The Crowd

The Wisemen, serious, large and imposing,
bear the inaccessible mystery of the
enigmas.
There is Ping! There is Pong! There is
Pang!

Diecimila anni al nostro Imperatore!
Gloria a te!

Ten thousand years to our Emperor!
Glory to you!

Die - ci-mi - la   an - ni   al nostro Impe - ra - to - re!

*Calaf stands at the base of the steps. Timur and Liù stand near him.
The Emperor addresses the Crowd, and then Calaf.*

L'Imperatore
Un giuramento atroce mi constringe
a tener fede al fosco patto.
E il santo scettro ch'io stringo gronda di
sangue.
Basta sangue! Giovine, va'!

The Emperor
I am obliged by an outrageous oath to be
faithful to this ominous covenant.
The sacred scepter that I bear drips with
blood.
Enough blood! Young man, go away!

Calaf
Figlio del Cielo, io chiedo d'affrontar la
prova!

Calaf
Son of Heaven, I request permission to
face the trial!

L'Imperatore
Fa ch'io possa morir senza portare
il peso della tua giovine vita!

The Emperor
You wish me to bear the guilt for your
young life after I die!

Calaf
Figlio del Cielo, io chiedo d'affrontar la
prova!

Calaf
Son of Heaven, I request permission to
face the trial!

L'Imperatore
Non voler che s'empia ancor d'orror la
Reggia, il mondo.

The Emperor
Don't wish even more wickedness on this
reign.

Calaf
Figlio del Cielo,
io chiedo d'affrontar la prova!

Calaf
Son of Heaven, I request permission to
confront the test!

L'Imperatore
Straniero, ebbro di morte!
E sia! Si compia il tuo destino!

The Emperor
Stranger, you are intoxicated with death!
Let it be! Fulfill your destiny!

La folla
Diecimila anni al nostro Imperatore!

The Crowd
Ten thousand years to our Emperor!

The Mandarin reads Turandot's decree to the Crowd.

Il Mandarino
Popolo di Pekino! La legge è questa:
Turandot, la pura, sposa sarà di chi,
di sangue regio, spieghi gli enigmi ch'ella
proporrà.
Ma chi affronta il cimento e vinto resta
porga alla scure la superba testa!

The Mandarin
People of Peking! This is the law.
The chaste Turandot will marry a man
of royal blood, who solves the riddles that
she proposes.
But the man who fails the test will have
his head impaled on the walls!

I ragazzi

Dal deserto al mar non odi mille voci
sospirar:
Principessa, scendi a me!
Tutto splenderà, splenderà, splenderà!

Boys

From desert to sea, you failed to hear
thousands of sighing voices calling you.
Princess, descend to me!
Everything will radiate! It will radiate!

Turandot rises from the throne. She looks coldly at Calaf,
and then solemnly addresses him.

Turandot

In questa reggia, or son mill'anni e mille,
un grido disperato risonò.
E quel grido, traverso stirpe e stirpe
qui nell'anima mia si rifugiò!

Turandot

In this realm, thousands and thousands of
years ago, an agonizing scream resounded.
And that shout, that was heard from
generation to generation, took refuge in
my soul!

Principessa Lou-Ling, ava dolce e serena
che regnavi nel tuo cupo silenzio
in gioia pura, e sfidasti inflessibile e sicura
l'aspro dominio, oggi rivivi in me!

Princess Lou-Ling, my gentle and placid
ancestress is revived in me. She was
undaunted and courageous to secure our
land, but now remains in gloomy silence
and chaste joy!

La folla

Fu quando il Re dei Tartari le sette sue
bandiere dispiegò.

The Crowd

It was when the Tartar king unleashed his
seven armies.

Turandot

Pure nel tempo che ciascun ricorda,
fu sgomento e terrore e rombo d'armi.

Turandot

Indeed it was a time that everyone
remembers; it was frightening and
terrifying, with the roar of armies.

Il regno vinto! E Lou-Ling,
la mia ava, trascinata da un uomo come te,
come te straniero, là nella notte atroce
dove si spense la sua fresca voce!

Her reign was defeated! And Lou-Ling,
my ancestor, was dragged before a man
like you, like you stranger. There in the
desperate night her wise voice was silenced!

La folla
Da secoli ella dorme nella sua tomba enorme.

The Crowd
It is for centuries that she rests in her imposing tomb.

Turandot
O Principi, che a lunghe carovane
d'ogni parte del mondo qui venite
a gettar la vostra sorte,
io vendico su voi, su voi quella purezza,
quel grido e quella morte!

Turandot
You Princes come here from every part of the world
to risk your fate,
I have vengeance for you, from that pure woman, from that shout and that death!

Mai nessun m'avrà!
L'orror di che l'uccise vivo nel cuor mi sta!

But no one will ever possess me!
The horror of her murder remains engraved within me!

No, no! Mai nessun m'avrà!

No, no! No one will ever possess me!

Largamente

Ah, rinasce in me l'orgoglio di tanta purità!
Straniero! Non tentar la fortuna!
Gli enigmi sono tre, la morte è una!

Ah, the pride of her purity is reborn within me!
Stranger! Don't tempt your luck!
There are three enigmas, but one death!

Gli e - nig - mi so - no tre, la mor - te è u - na!

Calaf
No, no! Gli enigmi sono tre, una è la vita!

Calaf
No, no! There are three enigmas, but one life!

La folla
Al Principe straniero offri la prova ardita, o Turandot! Turandot!

The Crowd
Turandot! Turandot! The unknown Prince offers to challenge your bold test!

Trumpets blare to announce the first riddle.

Turandot
Straniero, ascolta:
"Nella cupa notte vola un fantasma
iridescente. Sale e spiega l'ale sulla nera
infinita umanità.
Tutto il mondo l'invoca e tutto il mondo
l'implora. Ma il fantasma sparisce
coll'aurora per rinascere nel cuore.
Ed ogni notte nasce ed ogni giorno
muore!"

Turandot
Stranger, listen.
"An iridescent ghost flies in the dark night.
It spreads its wings on humanity! The
whole world invokes it, and the whole
world implores it! But the ghost disappears
with the dawn to be reborn in the heart!
Every night it is born, and every morning
it dies."

Calaf
Sì! Rinasce! Rinasce e in esultanza mi
porta via con sé, Turandot: La Speranza!

Calaf
Yes! Reborn! Reborn and triumphantly
brought me to you. Turandot: it is Hope!

I Sapienti
La Speranza! La Speranza! La Speranza!

The Wisemen
Hope! Hope! Hope!

Turandot
Sì, la speranza che delude sempre!

Turandot
Yes, hope that always deceives!

Turandot poses the second riddle.

"Guizza al pari di fiamma, e non è
fiamma. È talvolta delirio. È febbre
d'impeto e ardore! L'inerzia lo tramuta in
un languore.
Se ti perdi o trapassi, si rafredda.
Se sogni la conquista, avvampa, avvampa!
Ha una voce che trepido tu ascolti,
e del tramonto il vivido baglior!"

"Though not a flame, it darts like a flame!
It is a fire with intense heat! Its exertion
makes it weaken! If it is lost, you become
chilled!
If it is conquered, it inflames you!
You listen to its voice with fear,
and it glows like the setting sun!"

L'Imperatore
Non perderti, straniero!

The Emperor
Don't fail, stranger!

La folla
È per la vita! Parla!
Non perderti, straniero! Parla!

The Crowd
It is for your life! Speak!
Don't fail, stranger! Speak!

Liù
È per l'amore!

Liù
He does it for love!

Calaf

Sì, Principessa! Avvampa e insieme langue,
se tu mi guardi, nelle vene:
Il Sangue!

Calaf

Yes, Princess! It glows and at the same time languishes,
you can find it in the veins:
It is Blood!

I Sapienti

Il Sangue! Il Sangue! Il Sangue!

The Wisemen

Blood! Blood! Blood!

La folla

Coraggio, scioglitore degli enigmi!

The Crowd

Courage, solve the enigmas!

Turandot

Percuotete quei vili!

Turandot *(becoming anxious)*

Strike those vile ones!

Turandot poses the third riddle.

"Gelo che ti dà foco e dal tuo foco più gelo prende!
Candida ed oscura!
Se libero ti vuol ti fa più servo.
Se per servo t'accetta, ti fa Re!"

"The ice that inflames you and makes you more frigid! It is dispassionate and obscure! If you want to be free from it, it makes you subservient. If you serve it and it accepts you, you become king!

Su, straniero, ti sbianca la paura!
E ti senti perduto!
Su, straniero, il gelo che dà foco,
che cos'è?"

Rise, stranger, you're pale with fear!
And you sense defeat!
Rise, stranger, the ice that generates fire,
what is it?"

Calaf

La mia vittoria ormai t'ha data a me!
Il mio fuoco ti sgela: Turandot!

Calaf

Finally you have given me my victory!
It is my fire that melts you: it is Turandot!

I Sapienti

Turandot! Turandot! Turandot!

The Wisemen

Turandot! Turandot! Turandot!

La folla

Turandot! Turandot!
Gloria, gloria, o vincitore!
Ti sorrida la vita!
Ti sorrida l'amor!
Diecimila anni al nostro Imperatore!
Luce, Re di tutto il mondo!

The Crowd

Turandot! Turandot!
Glory, glory to the victor!
May life smile on you!
May love smile on you!
Ten thousand years to our Emperor!
Light, King of the entire world!

Agonizing over her defeat, Turandot pleads with the Emperor.

Turandot
Figlio del Cielo! Padre augusto!
No! Non gettar tua figlia
nelle braccia dello straniero!

Turandot
Son of Heaven! August father!
No! Don't cast your daughter into the arms
of the stranger!

L'Imperatore
È sacro il giuramento!

The Emperor
It is the sacred law!

Turandot
No, non dire! Tua figlia è sacra!
Non puoi donarmi a lui, a lui come una
schiava.

Turandot
No, don't say it! Your daughter is sacred!
You cannot give me to him, cast me to him
like I was a slave.

Ah, no! Tua figlia è sacra!
Non puoi donarmi a lui
come una schiava morente di vergogna!

Ah, no! Your daughter is sacred!
You cannot give me to him like a slave
dying of shame!

Turandot addresses Calaf.

Non guardarmi così!
Tu che irridi al mio orgoglio,
non guardarmi così!
Non sarò tua!
No, non sarò tua!
Non voglio, non voglio!

Don't look at me that way!
You mock my shame,
don't look at me that way!
I will never be yours!
No, I will never be yours!
It is not my will!

L'Imperatore
È sacro il giuramento!

The Emperor
It is a scared oath!

La folla
È sacro il giuramente!
Ha vinto, Principessa!
Offrì per te la vita!

The Crowd
It is the sacred law!
He has won, Princess!
He offered his life for you!

Turandot
Mai nessun m'avrà!

Turandot
No one will ever possess me!

La folla
Sia premio al suo ardimento!

The Crowd
You are the prize of his boldness!

Turandot
Mi vuoi nelle tue braccia a forza,
riluttante, fremente?

Turandot
Do you wish in your arms by force,
cold and unwilling?

La folla
È sacro, è sacro, è sacro il giuramente, è sacro!

The Crowd
It is sacred, it is the sacred law!

Calaf
No, no, Principessa altera!
Ti voglio ardente d'amor!

Calaf
No, no, proud Princess!
I want your love to be ardent!

La folla
Coraggioso! Audace!
Coraggioso! O forte!

The Crowd
Courageous! Dauntless!
Courageous! Oh what strength!

Moderto sostenuto

Calaf
Tre enigmi m'hai proposto, e tre ne sciolsi.
Uno soltanto a te ne proporrò:
Il mio nome non sai. Dimmi il mio nome.
Dimmi il mio nome prima dell'alba,
e all'alba morirò…

Calaf
You proposed three riddles, and I solved the three riddles.
I will propose one riddle for you.
You do not know my name.
Tell me my name before sunrise,
and at sunrise I will die.

L'Imperatore
Il cielo voglia che col primo sole mio figliolo tu sia!

The Emperor
The Heavens may wish that at sunrise you will become my son!

La folla
Ai tuoi piedi ci prostriam, Luce,
Re di tutto il mondo!
Per la tua saggezza,
per la tua bontà ci doniamo a te, lieti in umiltà,
a te salga il nostro amor!

The Crowd *(to the Emperor)*
We prostrate ourselves at your feet, Light,
King of the entire world!
We sacrifice ourselves to you, happily and humbly, because of your wisdom and goodness,
and may our love rise to you!

Diecimila anni al nostro Imperatore!
A te, erede di Hien-Wang noi gridiam:
Diecimila anni al nostro Imperatore!
Alte, alte le bandiere!
Gloria a te! Gloria a te!

Ten thousand years to our Emperor!
To you, hero of Hien-Wang we shout.
Ten thousand years to our Emperor!
Raise the banners!
Glory to you! Glory to you!

ACT III - Scene 1

The garden of Turandot's palace. It is night.

Gli araldi	**The Heralds**
Così comanda Turandot:	Thus Turandot has commanded:
"Questa notte nessun dorma in Pekino!"	"On this night no one sleeps in Peking!"
La folla	**The Crowd**
Nessun dorma! Nessun dorma!	No one sleeps! No one sleeps!
Gli araldi	**The Heralds**
"Pena la morte, il nome dell'ignoto	"On the pain of death, the stranger's name
sia rivelato prima del mattino!"	must be revealed by morning!"
La folla	**The Crowd**
Pena la morte! Pena la morte!	The pain of death! The pain of death!

Andante sostenuto
CALAF

Calaf	**Calaf**
Nessun dorma! Nessun dorma!	No one sleeps! No one sleeps!
Tu pure, o Principessa,	You, chaste Princess,
nella tua fredda stanza guardi le stelle	from your cold room, look at the stars that
che tremano d'amore e di speranza.	tremble with love and hope.
Ma il mio mistero è chiuso in me,	But my mystery is locked within me,
il nome mio nessun saprà!	and no one will learn my name!
No, no, sulla tua bocca lo dirò,	No, no, your mouth will say it,
quando la luce splenderà.	when the light shines.
Ed il mio bacio scioglierà	And my kiss will dissolve that silence
il silenzio che ti fa mia.	that has made you mine.
Le donne	**The Women**
Il nome suo nessun saprà.	No one will know his name.
E noi dovrem, ahimè, morir, morir!	And alas, we must die!

Calaf
Dilegua, o notte! Tramontate, stelle!
All'alba vincerò!
Vincerò!

Calaf
Vanish, oh night! Trembling stars!
At sunrise I will be victorious!
I will be victorious!

Ping, Pong, Pang
Tu che guardi le stelle,
abbassa gli occhi.
La nostra vita è in tuo potere!

Ping, Pong, Pang
You who look to the stars,
lower your eyes.
We have power over your life!

Ping
Uddisti il bando?
Per le vie di Pekino ad ogni porta batte la
morte e grida: il nome!

Ping
Did you hear the announcement?
Throughout Peking, every door is struck
with death and shouts: his name!

Pong, Pang
Il nome!

Pong, Pang
His name!

Ping, Pong, Pang
O sangue!

Ping, Pong, Pang
Oh blood!

Calaf
Che volete da me?

Calaf
What do you want with me?

Ping, Pong, Pang
Di' tu che vuoi? È l'amore che cerchi?
Ebbene, prendi!
Guarda, son belle, son belle fra luccenti
veli.

Ping, Pong, Pang
What do you want? You seek love?
Well, take it!
Look, they are beautiful, beautiful
between the sparkling veils.

Pong, Pang
Corpi flessuosi.

Pong, Pang
Fleshy bodies.

Ping
Tutte ebbrezze e promesse d'amplessi
prodigiosi!

Ping
All intoxicated and with promises of
wonderful embraces!

Calaf
No! No!

Calaf
No! No!

Ping, Pong, Pang
Che vuoi? Ricchezze?
Tutti i tesori a te!
Rompon la notte nera queste fulgide
gemme!

Ping, Pong, Pang
What do you want? Riches?
All treasures are for you!
The dark night overflows with these
resplendent gems!

Fuochi azzurri! Verdi splendori!
Pallidi giacinti! Le vampe rosse dei rubini!
Sono gocciole d'astri!
Prendi! È tutto tuo!

Blue fires! Green splendors!
Pallid hyacinths! The fiery red of rubies!
They are the teardrops of the stars!
Take them! It is all for you!

Calaf
No! Nessuna ricchezza! No!

Calaf
No! No riches! No!

Ping, Pong, Pang
Vuoi la gloria?
Noi ti farem fuggir e andrai lontano
con le stelle verso imperi favolosi!

Ping, Pong, Pang
Do you want glory?
We can make you flee and go far with the
stars toward the mythical empire!

La folla
Fuggi!

The Crowd
Flee!

Le donne
Va' lontano, va' lontano!

The Women
Go far away!

La folla
Fuggi! Va' lontano, e noi ci salviam!

The Crowd
Flee! Go far away, and we will be saved!

Calaf
Alba, vieni! Quest'incubo dissolvi!

Calaf
Sunrise, come! Let this nightmare end!

Ping
Straniero, tu non sai di che cosa è capace
la Crudele.

Ping
Stranger, you don't know how much
cruelty she is capable of.

Ping, Pong, Pang
Tu non sai quali orrendi martiri la China
inventi.
Se tu rimani e non ci sveli il nome siam
perduti.
L'insonne non perdona!

Ping, Pong, Pang
You don't know how many martyrs China
has created.
We are lost if you remain and don't reveal
your name.
The sleepless offer no pardon!

La folla
Sarà martirio orrendo!
I ferri aguzzi! L'irte ruote!
Il caldo morso delle tenaglie!
La morte a sorso a sorso!
Non farci morire!

The Crowd
It will be a horrendous martyrdom!
Sharp steel! Pointed wheels!
The hot sting of pincers!
Sipping death!
Don't force us to die!

Calaf
Inutili preghiere! Inutili minacce!
Crollasse il mondo, voglio Turandot!

Calaf
Useless prayers! Useless menaces!
Let the world collapses, I want Turandot!

La folla
Non l'avrai!
No, non l'avrai!
Morrai prima di noi! Tu maledetto!
Morrai prima di noi,
tu spietato, crudele!
Parla, il nome, il nome, il nome!

The Crowd
You won't possess her!
No, you won't possess her!
You will die before us! You are cursed!
You will die before us,
you are pitiless, cruel!
Speak, the name, the name!

A group of soldiers drag in Timur and Liù.

Gli sgherri
Eccolo il nome! È qua! È qua!

Soldiers
Here you'll learn the name! It is here.

Calaf
Costor non sanno!
Ignorano il mio nome!

Calaf
They know nothing!
They're ignorant of my name!

Ping
Sono il vecchio e la giovane
che ier sera parlavano con te!

Ping
They are the old man and the young girl
who spoke with you last evening!

Calaf
Lasciateli!

Calaf
Let them go!

Ping
Conoscono il segreto!
Dove li avete colti?

Ping
They know the secret!
Where did you find them?

Gli sgherri
Mentre erravano là, presso le mura!

Soldiers
While they were over there, near the wall!

Turandot appears.

Ping, Pong, Pang, la folla
Principessa!

Ping, Pong, Pang, the Crowd
Princess!

Ping
Principessa divina! Il nome dell'ignoto
sta chiuso in queste bocche silenti.
E abbiamo ferri per schiodar quei denti e
uncini abbiamo per strappar quel nome!

Ping *(pointing to Timur and Liù)*
Divine Princess! The name of the stranger
remains in these silent mouths.
And we have tools and hooks to remove
their nails and teeth to tear the name from
them!

Turandot
Sei pallido, straniero!

Turandot *(addressing Calaf)*
You are pale, stranger!

Calaf
Il tuo sgomento vede il pallor dell'alba sul mio volto.
Costor non mi conoscono!

Calaf
Your fear sees the pallor of sunrise on my face.
They do not know me!

Turandot
Vedremo! Su, parla, vecchio!
Io voglio ch'egli parli! Il nome!

Turandot
We shall see! Rise, speak, old man!
I want you to speak! His name!

Liù
Il nome che cercate io sola so!

Liù
I alone know the name you seek!

La folla
La vita è salva, l'incubo svanì!

The Crowd
Life is saved, the nightmare ended!

Calaf
Tu non sai nulla, schiava!

Calaf
You know nothing, slave!

Liù
Io so il suo nome.
M'è suprema delizia tenerlo segreto e possederlo io sola!

Liù
I know his name.
But it is a supreme joy to be the only one to possess that secret!

La folla
Sia legata! Sia straziata!
Perché parli! Perché muoia!

The Crowd
Tie her! Torture her!
Why not speak! Why should you die!

Calaf
Sconterete le sue lagrime!
Sconterete i suoi tormenti!

Calaf
Atone for your tears!
Atone for your torment!

Turandot
Tenetelo!

Turandot
Hold him!

Liù
Signor, non parlerò!

Liù
My lord, I won't speak!

Ping
Quel nome!

Ping
His name!

Liù
No!

Liù
No!

Ping
Quel nome!

Ping
His name!

Liù
La tua serva chiede perdono,
ma obbedir non può! Ah!

Liù
Your slave asks pardon, but they cannot
make me obey! Ah!

Timur
Perché gridi!

Timur
Why do you shout!

Calaf
Lasciatela!

Calaf
Let her free!

Liù
No, non grido più! Non mi fan male!
No, nessun mi tocca!
Stringete, ma chiudetemi la bocca
ch'ei non mi senta! Non resisto più!

Liù
No, don't shout! They can't harm me!
No, no one touch me!
Crush me, but I close my mouth so I won't
feel! I can't resist any more!

La folla
Parla! Il suo nome!

The Crowd
Speak! His name!

Turandot
Sia lasciata! Parla!

Turandot
Free her! Speak!

Liù
Piuttosto morrò!

Liù
Soon I will die!

Turandot
Chi pose tanta forza nel tuo cuore?

Turandot
What powerful force lies in your heart?

Liù
Principessa, l'amore!

Liù
Princess, it is love!

Turandot
L'amore?

Turandot
Love?

Liù
Tanto amore segreto e inconfessato,
grande così che questi strazi son dolcezze
per me
perché ne faccio dono al mio Signore.
Perché, tacendo, io gli do, gli do il tuo
amore.
Te gli do, Principessa, e perdo tutto!

Persino l'impossibile speranza!
Legatemi! Straziatemi!

Liù
So much secret and unavowed love,
so great that this torment is sweetness for
me
because I give it as a gift to my lord.
Because, being silent, I give him his love.

I give it to you, Princess, and I lose
everything!
Even the impossible hope!
Tie me! Torture me!

Tormenti e spasimi date a me,
ah, come offerta suprema del mio amore!

Those tortures and pains,
are the offerings of my supreme love!

Turandot
Strappatele il segreto!

Turandot
Tear the secret from her!

Ping
Chiamate Pu-Tin-Pao!

Ping
Call Pu-Tin-Pao!

Calaf
No! Maledetto! Maledetto!

Calaf
No! Curse you!

La folla
Il boia! Il boia! Il boia!

The Crowd
The executioner!

Ping
Sia messa alla tortura!

Ping
Start the torture!

La folla
Alla tortura! Sì, il boia!
Parli! Alla tortura!

The Crowd
The torture! Yes, the executioner!
Speak! Use torture!

Liù
Più non resisto! Ho paura di me!
Lasciatemi passare!

Liù
I can't resist any more! I have fear!
Let me pass!

La folla
Parla! Parla!

The Crowd
Speak! Speak!

Liù
Sì, Principessa, ascoltami!

Liù
Yes, Princess, listen to me!

Andantino mosso
LIÙ

Tu,   che di gel   sei   cin - ta,

Tu che di gel sei cinta,
da tanta fiamma vinta, l'amerai anche tu!
Prima di questa aurora io chiudo stanca gli
occhi, perché egli vinca ancora.
Ei vinca ancor!
Per non vederlo più!

You, wrapped in ice, flames have
defeated you, and you will also love!
Before sunrise I close my tired eyes,
because he has been victorious.
And love will be the victor!
And I will never see him again!

Liù dies.

La folla
Ah! Parla! Parla! Il nome! Il nome!

The Crowd
Ah! Speak! Speak! His name! His name!

Calaf
Ah! Tu sei morta, o mia piccola Liù!

Calaf
Ah! You are dead, my little Liù!

Timur
Liù! Sorgi!
È l'ora chiara d'ogni risveglio.
È l'alba, o mia Liù.
Apri gli occhi, colomba!

Timur
Liù! Rise!
It is the hour of awakening.
It is sunrise, my Liù.
Open your eyes, my dove!

Ping
Alzati, vecchio! È morta!

Ping
Get up, old man! She is dead!

Timur
Ah! Delitto orrendo! L'espieremo tutti!
L'anima offesa si vendicherà!

Timur
Ah! Horrible crime! We condemn you all!
The offended soul will be avenged!

La folla
Ombra dolente, non farci del male!
Ombra sdegnosa, perdona, perdona!

The Crowd
Sorrowful spirit, don't condemn us!
Indignant spirit, pardon!

Timur
Liù, bontà! Liù, dolcezza!
Ah, camminiamo insieme un'altra volta
così, con la tua mano nella mia mano.
Dove vai ben so.
Ed io ti seguirò per posare a te vicino
nella notte che non ha mattino!

Timur
Liù, kind one! Liù, gentle one!
Ah, we'll travel together another time
with your hand in mine.
I know well where you go.
And I will follow you to be near you in that
darkness that has no morning!

Ping, Pong, Pang
Svegliato s'è qui dentro il vecchio
ordigno, il cuore, e mi tormenta!
Ah, per la prima volta
al vedere la morte non sogghigno!
Quella fanciulla spenta pesa
sopra il mio cuor come un macigno!

Ping, Pong, Pang
One is aroused by his loss,
and it agonizes and torments me!
Ah, for the first time I don't scorn the sight
of death!
That young girl's death weighs on my
heart like a heavy stone!

La folla
Liù, bontà, perdona, perdona!
Liù, bontà, Liù, dolcezza, dormi!
Oblia! Liù! Poesia!

The Crowd
Liù, kind one, pardon, pardon!
Liù, kind one, Liù, gentle one, sleep!
Oblivion! Liù! Poetry!

ACT III - Scene 2

Calaf

Principessa di morte! Principessa di gelo!
Dal tuo tragico cielo scendi giù sulla terra!
Ah, solleva quel velo!
Guarda, crudele,
quel purissimo sangue che fu sparso per
te!

Calaf

Princess of death! Princess of ice!
Descend to earth from your tragic heaven!
Ah, raise your veil!
Look, cruel one,
at that pure blood that was shed for you!

Turandot

Che mai osi, straniero!
Cosa umana non sono!
Son la figlia del Cielo
libera e pura.
Tu stringi il mio freddo velo ma l'anima è
lassù!

Turandot

What do you dare, stranger!
I am not a human being!
I am the daughter of Heaven,
free and chaste.
You may pierce my cold exterior, but
never my soul!

Calaf

La tua anima è in alto, ma il tuo corpo è
vicino!
Con le mani brucianti stringerò
i lembi d'oro del tuo manto stellato.
La mia bocca fremente premerò su di te.

Calaf

Your soul is in the Heavens, but your body
is near!
I will hold the golden edges of your
sparkling dress with my burning hands.
I will place my throbbing mouth on yours.

Turandot

Non profanarmi!

Turandot

Don't malign me!

Calaf

Ah, sentirti viva!

Calaf

Ah, feel the essence of life!

Turandot

Indietro!

Turandot

Go away from me!

Calaf

Il gelo tuo è menzogna!

Calaf

Your ice is a lie!

Turandot

No, mai nessun m'avrà!

Turandot

No, no one will ever possess me!

Calaf

Ti voglio mia!

Calaf

I love you!

Turandot
Dell'ava lo strazio non si rinnoverà!
Ah, no!

Turandot
Don't renew the suffering of my ancestress!
Ah, no!

Calaf
Ti voglio mia!

Calaf
I love you!

Turandot
Non mi toccar, straniero!
È un sacrilegio!

Turandot
Don't touch me, stranger!
It is a sacrilege!

Calaf
No, il bacio tuo mi dà l'eternità!

Calaf
No, your kiss will give me eternity!

Turandot
Sacrilegio!
Che è mai di me? Perduta!

Turandot *(Calaf kisses Turandot)*
Sacrilege!
What did you do to me? I am lost!

Calaf
Mio fiore! Oh, mio fiore mattutino!
Mio fiore, ti respiro!
I seni tuoi di giglio,
ah, treman sul mio petto!
Già ti sento mancare di dolcezza,
tutta bianca nel tuo manto d'argento.

Calaf
My flower! Oh, my morning flower!
My flower, I breathe your essence!
Your breast is like lilies,
ah, my chest trembles!
Already I feel you wanting gentleness,
all white in your silver dress.

Turandot
Come vincesti?

Turandot
How did you defeat me?

Calaf
Piangi?

Calaf
Are you crying?

Turandot
È l'alba! Turandot tramonta!

Turandot
It is sunrise! Turandot's sunset!

I ragazzi
L'alba! Luce e vita! Tutto è puro!

Boys
Sunrise! Light and life! All is chaste!

Gli uomini
L'alba! Luce e vita! Principessa,
che dolcezza nel tuo pianto!

The Men
Sunrise! Light and life! Princess,
what gentleness in your weeping!

Calaf
È l'alba! E amore nasce col sole!

Calaf
It is sunrise! Love is born with the sun!

I ragazzi
Tutto è santo! Che dolcezza nel tuo
pianto!

Boys
All is sacred! What gentleness in your
weeping!

Turandot
Che nessun mi veda, la mia gloria è finita!

Turandot
May no one see me, my glory is finished!

Calaf
No! Essa incomincia!

Calaf
No! It just begins!

Turandot
Onta su me!

Turandot
I have shame!

Calaf
Miracolo! La tua gloria risplende
nell'incanto del primo bacio, del primo
pianto!

Calaf
It is a miracle! Your glory sparkles in the
enchantment of the first kiss, the first kiss!

Turandot
Del primo pianto.
Ah! Del primo pianto!
Sì, straniero, quando sei giunto,
con angoscia ho sentito il brivido fatale
di questo mal supremo.

Turandot
From the first tear.
Ah! From the first tear!
Yes, stranger, when you arrived, I felt
anguish and the fatal quiver
of this supreme evil.

Quanti ho visto morire per me!
E li ho spregiati. Ma ho temuto te!
C'era negli occhi tuoi la luce degli eroi.
C'era negli occhi tuoi la superba certezza.
E t'ho odiato per quella!
E per quella t'ho amato!

I saw how much you wanted to die for me!
And I despised you. But I feared you!
In your eyes I saw the light of a hero.
In your eyes a superb assurance.
And I hated you for that!
And I loved you for that!

Tormentata e divisa fra due terrori uguali:
vincerti o esser vinta.
E vinta sono!
Ah! Vinta, più che dall'alta prova,
da questa febbre che mi vien da te!

I was tormented and divided by two equal
terrors: to defeat you or be defeated.
And I am defeated!
Ah! Defeated by the burning passion that
you instill in me.

Calaf
Sei mia! Mia!

Calaf
You are mine! Mine!

Turandot
Questo chiedevi. Ora lo sai.
Più grande vittoria non voler!
Parti, straniero, col tuo mister!

Turandot
You yearned for this. Now you know.
Don't wish for a greater victory!
Leave, stranger, leave with your mystery!

Calaf
Il mio mistero? Non ne ho più!
Sei mia!
Tu che tremi se ti sfioro!
Tu che sbianchi se ti bacio puoi perdermi
se vuoi!
Il mio nome e la vita insiem ti dono!
Io sono Calaf, figlio di Timur!

Calaf
My mystery? I no longer have it!
You are mine!
You trembled when I barely touched you!
You became pale when I kissed you and
you now wish me to leave!
My name and life are one, I give both to you!
I am Calaf, son of Timur!

Turandot
So il tuo nome!
So il tuo nome!

Turandot
I now know your name!
I now know your name!

Calaf
La mia gloria è il tuo amplesso!

Calaf
My glory is your embrace!

Turandot
Odi! Squillan le trombe!

Turandot
Listen! The trumpets blare!

Calaf
La mia vita è il tuo bacio!

Calaf
My life is your kiss!

Turandot
Ecco! È l'ora!
È l'ora della prova!

Turandot
Now! It is the hour!
It is the hour of proof!

Calaf
Non la temo!

Calaf
I do not fear!

Turandot
Ah! Calaf, davanti al popolo con me!

Turandot
Calaf, come with me before the people!

Calaf
Hai vinto tu!

Calaf
You are the victor!

La folla
Diecimila anni al nostro Imperatore!

The Crowd
Ten thousand years to our Emperor!

Turandot
Padre augusto, conosco il nome dello
straniero!
Il suo nome... è Amor!

Turandot
August father, I know the name of the
stranger!
His name....is Love!

La folla

Amor! O sole! Vita! Eternità!
Luce del mondo e amore!
Ride e canta nel sole l'infinità nostra
felicità!
Gloria a te! Gloria a te! Gloria!

The Crowd

Love! Oh sun! Life! Eternity!
The light of the world is love!
The sun smiles and sings of our infinite
happiness!
Glory to you! Glory to you! Glory!

Made in the USA
Monee, IL
14 April 2022